I ♥ Craft

CARDS
and
WRAPPING PAPER

Rita Storey

Franklin Watts
Published in Great Britain in 2017
by The Watts Publishing Group

Series editor: Sarah Peutrill

Packaged for Franklin Watts by Storeybooks
rita@storeybooks.co.uk
Designer: Rita Storey
Editor: Sarah Ridley
Crafts made by: Rita Storey
Photography: Tudor Photography, Banbury
www.tudorphotography.co.uk

Printed in China

Dewey classification: 745.5'941
ISBN: 978 1 4451 5498 5

Cover images: Tudor Photography, Banbury

Franklin Watts
An imprint of
Hachette Children's Group
Part of The Watts Publishing Group
Carmelite House
50 Victoria Embankment
London EC4Y 0DZ

An Hachette UK Company
www.hachette.co.uk
www.franklinwatts.co.uk

FSC
www.fsc.org
MIX
Paper from
responsible sources
FSC® C104740

Before you start

Some of the projects in this book require scissors, pins or a craft knife. When using these things we would recommend that children are supervised by a responsible adult.

Please note: keep homemade cards away from babies and small children. They cannot be tested for safety.

Contents

Crazy Frame Card

Turn a picture of a cute animal or a pop star into a colourful card. Make it unique by decorating it with a collection of odds and ends from around the house.

You will need:

* sheet of green card, 297mm x 148mm
* ruler * pencil
* craft knife (ask an adult to use it)
* A4 sheet of yellow card
* glue and spreader
* picture or photo
* sticky tape
* ribbon, patterned wrapping paper, feathers, buttons, stick-on craft jewels, sweet wrappers

Fold

Opening

1 Fold the card in half along the longest side. With the opening on the right, use the ruler to mark points 3cm in from each corner. Draw lines, using the ruler, to join up the points to create a frame shape.

2 Open out the card. Ask an adult to cut along the pencil lines with the craft knife as shown.

3 Place the green card on top of the yellow card, matching up the corners. Draw along the inside of the frame using a pencil.

4 Use the ruler to mark points 1cm out from the pencil lines. Draw lines, using the ruler, to join up the points and cut along these outer lines. This yellow card will form the backing for your picture.

5 Cut out your picture. Glue it onto the yellow card.

6 Open out the card. With the picture facing out through the frame, use sticky tape to attach the yellow card to the green. Close the card.

7 Cut the wrapping paper into a zig-zag shape. Glue it onto the card under the picture. Cut a strip of ribbon the same width as the card. Glue it above the picture.

8 This card uses stickers, buttons, a sweet wrapper, feathers and a piece of ribbon to finish it off. Decorate your card as you wish, using available materials.

Monster Hug Card

This adorable monster has long fold-out arms to deliver a monster of a hug.

You will need:

* pencil and 2 sheets of thin white paper (for tracing the templates)
* sewing pins
* fur fabric
* fabric scissors
* A3 sheet of blue card
* fabric glue and spreader
* A4 sheet of yellow paper
* strip of yellow card, 59cm x 4cm
* sticky tape
* 2 googly eyes
* felt-tip pen

1 Use thin white paper and a pencil to trace the body template on page 29. Cut it out and pin it onto the fur fabric. Cut out your fabric monster shape. Remove the pins and template and set to one side.

Fold

2 Fold the blue card in half along the longest side. Place the top of the template on the fold. Draw around the template and cut it out.

3 Open out the shape.

You could draw around your own hands instead of the hand template in step 5.

6

4 Spread glue onto the smooth side of the fur monster. Glue it in place on the front of the card, matching the edges.

5 Use thin white paper and a pencil to trace the hand template on page 29. Cut it out. Draw around the template on the yellow paper twice. Cut out two paper hands.

6 Tape a paper hand to each end of the long strip of yellow card.

7 Tape the centre of the long strip onto the back of the monster card.

8 Glue the googly eyes onto the front of the monster card.

9 Trace the speech bubble template on page 28 and cut out a blue card speech bubble. Write your own message and glue it in place.

Here is a big hug from me!

Pop-up Ghost Card

This spooky card would make a great Hallowe'en party invitation.

You will need:

* 2 x A4 sheets of thin purple card
* A4 sheet of yellow paper
* bowl, approx 150mm across
* pencil and thin white paper (for tracing the templates)
* scissors
* PVA glue and spreader
* A4 sheet of black card
* A4 sheet of white card
* black felt-tip pen
* stick-on stars

Once you have made this pop-up card, you could use the same skills to make cards for other occasions.

1 Fold both sheets of purple card in half along the longest side.

2 Draw around the bowl onto the yellow paper. Cut out the paper circle.

3 Glue the paper circle onto the inside of one piece of folded card, as shown.

Fold 4cm 4cm 4cm

4 Use the pencil and thin white paper to trace the castle and bat templates on page 28. Place the templates on the black card and draw around them. Cut out the shapes.

5 Glue the castle and bats in place, as shown.

6 Fold the card shut. Use scissors to make two 4-cm long cuts in the folded edge, 4cm from the right-hand edge and 4cm apart. Fold back the paper between the cuts. Crease the fold.

8 Fold the card shut. Cover the outside of the card with a thin layer of glue. Put it inside the other sheet of folded purple card. Press flat and leave it to dry.

7 Open out the card. Push the piece of card up between the cut lines. It should look like the picture above.

9 Use the template on page 28 to cut out a ghost from the white card. Draw on eyes with the black felt-tip pen. Glue the ghost to the pop-up fold that sticks out, as shown. Stick on the stars (see main picture, right).

Write your message here.

9

Stained Glass Card

This card looks good with light shining through it, just like a stained glass window. Place it near a window or a lamp to see it at its best.

You will need:

* ⋆ sheet of thick red paper, 297mm x 148mm
* ⋆ sheet of thin black paper, 145mm x145mm
* ⋆ pencil and ruler
* ⋆ scissors
* ⋆ PVA glue and paintbrush
* ⋆ clear plastic, 145mm x 145mm (cut from a clear plastic folder for example)
* ⋆ masking tape
* ⋆ torn up pieces of coloured tissue paper

Make an envelope out of an A4 piece of paper. See pages 26 – 27 for instructions.

1 Fold the thick red paper in half along the longest side. Measure points 1cm in from each corner and join them up to create a pencil line frame as shown in the picture above.

2 Open out the card and cut out the middle section. Put the card to one side until you reach step 9.

3 Fold the square of black paper in half from top to bottom.

A

B

C

4 Fold it in half again, as shown.

5 Fold the paper again, from the folded corner to the corner diagonally opposite, as shown.

6 Use scissors to cut off the top corner (A), as shown. Cut a triangular shape out of one side (B). Cut a semi-circular shape from the opposite side (C).

7 Carefully unfold the paper to reveal the cut-out holes. Use pieces of masking tape to fix the square of plastic onto one side of the paper.

8 Turn the paper over. Glue pieces of coloured tissue to cover the cut-out holes. Leave everything to dry. Peel off the masking tape and plastic.

9 Open out the red card. Paste glue onto the inside of the paper frame. With the untidy side on the inside, press the decorated black paper in place. Leave it to dry.

11

Rocket Card

Pull the tab for lift-off with this colourful moon rocket birthday card.

1 Fold the black card in half along the shorter side to create a tall card.

You will need:

* black card, 198mm x 210mm
* A4 sheet of thin white paper
* A4 sheet of thin blue paper
* thick white paper, 85mm x 210mm
* pencil
* scissors
* glue
* 5-mm wide, double-sided sticky tape
* pink paper
* yellow paper
* red paper
* photograph of your friend that fits inside the centre circle of the window
* fine black felt-tip pen
* stick-on craft jewels

2 Using the thin white paper and a pencil, trace the rocket template on page 29 and cut it out. Draw around the template on the blue paper. Cut it out.

3 Open out the black card. Glue the rocket onto the front. Cut out the inside of the window. Ask an adult for help if you find this difficult.

4 Stick a strip of double-sided tape to the inside of the long side of the card. Peel off the backing and close the card so that it sticks together.

5 Trace the nose cone and window templates on page 29 onto thin white paper. Use the templates to cut out a pink window and a yellow nose cone. Glue them onto the card and stick the craft jewels around the window.

6 Trace the flame templates on page 29 onto thin white paper. Use the templates to cut out red and yellow paper flames. Stick them one on top of the other onto the thick white paper, 1cm from the bottom, as shown.

7 With the flames facing up, slide the white paper inside the card. Leave 1cm of white paper showing at the bottom. Draw a circle inside the window.

8 Gently, slide the white paper out of the card until the circle disappears. Draw another pencil circle inside the window.

HAPPY BIRTHDAY

9 Slide the white paper out of the card. Cut out a picture of your friend to fit inside the top circle and glue it in place. Write a message in the lower circle.

10 Slide the strip of paper inside the card again, with the picture, the message and the flames facing up. The message will appear in the window. When you pull the paper tab, the picture will appear in the window.

Sweet Flower Card

This flower has a sweet centre and a butterfly you can eat. It is a card and a gift rolled into one.

You will need:

* thick blue card, 297mm x 148.5mm
* craft knife (ask an adult to use it)
* ruler * scissors
* pen and thin white paper (for the template)
* yellow paper * green paper
* pencil/compass
* red paper
* PVA glue and spreader
* lolly
* double-sided sticky tape
* pink paper
* wrapped sweet
* 2 googly eyes
* small orange pom-pom (from a craft shop)
* felt-tip pen

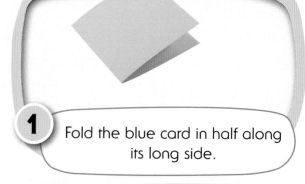

1 Fold the blue card in half along its long side.

2 Open up the card. Ask an adult to use the craft knife and the ruler to make two slits in the front of the card, as shown.

3 Use the pen and thin white paper to trace the flower template on page 32. Cut it out and draw around it on the yellow paper. Cut out a yellow paper flower.

4 Glue the yellow flower onto the card, just above the slits.

5 Use the ruler to set the compass to 2cm. Now use the compass to draw a circle on the red paper. Cut it out.

6 Glue the red circle onto the centre of the yellow flower. Push the lolly stick through the slit in the card, as shown.

7 Trace the grass template on page 32. Use it to cut out green paper grass.

8 Use double-sided sticky tape to fix the paper grass in place, as shown, with the lolly stick underneath the paper grass.

9 Trace the butterfly wings template on page 32 and cut it out. Use it to cut out pink paper butterfly wings.

10 Fold the paper wings in half and use double-sided sticky tape to attach them to the wrapped sweet, as shown. Glue the pom-pom to the sweet.

11 Glue the googly eyes onto the pom-pom. Fix the sweet to the card with a small piece of double-sided sticky tape.

Swimming Fish Card

These colourful fish are swimming in their own goldfish bowl. Send someone a birthday fish-wish!

You will need:

* pencil and thin white paper (for tracing the template)

* scissors * white paper * light blue card

* PVA glue and paintbrush

* small blue beads

AND

For the goldfish:

* thick orange paper * 2 googly eyes

* 2 x 15cm lengths of white embroidery thread

* sticky tape

For the patterned fish:

* thick patterned paper

* 2 googly eyes

* 2 x 15cm lengths of white embroidery thread

* sticky tape

1 Use thin white paper and a pencil to trace the goldfish bowl template on pages 30 – 31. Cut it out. Draw around it on the light blue card.

2 Cut along your pencil lines. Now your card should look like this.

3 Spread some glue along the bottom of the card, as shown.

4 Sprinkle on some blue beads and leave them to dry. Shake off any loose beads.

5 Trace the water template on page 31 onto white paper and cut it out. Glue the paper water shape in place, as shown.

6 Trace the fish template on page 31 and cut it out. Draw around the fish template on orange paper and cut it out. Fold across the fish tails and then open the paper out again.

7 Brush glue onto one side of one fish and place the thread, as shown, onto the glue.

8 Fold the other half over to trap the thread inside. Stick a googly eye on each side of the fish.

9 Repeat steps 6 – 8 to make a second paper fish using patterned paper.

10 Tape the threads to the top and bottom of the frame, as shown. Fold the card in half so that it can stand up.

Marbled Wrapping

This simple technique makes beautiful paper to wrap up small gifts and make them look special.

You will need:

* shaving foam   * wooden spoon
* large baking tray or foil roasting dish
* bottles of yellow, blue, green and red food colouring
* kitchen fork
* 1 x sheet of A3 paper for each print
* kitchen roll
* clothes pegs   * length of string tied between two points

1 Use the wooden spoon to spread a thin layer of shaving foam across the bottom of a baking tray.

2 Drop dots of food colouring onto the surface of the shaving foam. Use the fork to create swirling patterns of colour.

3 Carefully place a sheet of paper on top of the shaving foam.

4 Gently smooth the paper down so that it picks up the swirling colours.

5 Carefully lift off the paper. Wipe away any extra shaving foam with a piece of kitchen roll.

6 Hang your sheet of marbled paper up to dry using a peg.

7 Repeat steps 3 – 6 to get a similar piece of wrapping paper or mix the colours up for a change. Add another colour or start again, to make a completely different pattern.

8 If you use white card instead of paper, you can make cards and gift tags to match your wrapping paper.

Printed Wrapping

Wrap gifts in style with your own printed wrapping paper.

You will need:

* medium-sized uncooked potato
* kitchen knife (ask an adult to use it)
* kitchen roll

For the heart print paper:

* green felt-tip pen
* red paint
* paintbrush
* large sheet of brown parcel paper

For the elephant print paper:

* fine tip black felt-tip pen
* pink paint
* paintbrush
* large sheet of white paper

If you would like to make Christmas wrapping paper, cut your wedge of potato into the shape of a Christmas tree or a star.

Potato print hearts

1 Ask an adult to cut a 2-cm wedge from a potato. Dry one side of the potato with kitchen roll. Draw a simple heart shape onto it.

2 Ask an adult to use a kitchen knife to cut around the heart shape.

3 Dab red paint on one side of the potato heart.

Potato print elephants

4 Press the potato heart onto the brown paper. Lift it off. Move it down and print again. When the prints get faint, add more paint. When you are happy with your design, leave it to dry.

1 Ask an adult to cut a 2-cm wedge from a potato. Dry one side of the potato with kitchen roll. Use the template on page 32 or copy the elephant shape shown here onto the potato.

2 Ask an adult to use a kitchen knife to cut around the elephant shape.

3 Dab pink paint on one side of the potato elephant.

4 Press the potato elephant onto the white paper. Lift it off. Move it to a different position and print again. When the prints get faint, add more paint. Leave the printed paper to dry.

5 Use the black felt-tip pen to draw an eye, an ear, a tail and toes, copying the picture shown here. Repeat for each elephant.

You will need:

For the flower print paper:

* wire scouring pads * large sheet of white paper

* red paint * saucer * pink paint

* green felt-tip pen

For the fingerprint chicks paper:

* yellow paint * saucer * scrap paper

* large sheet of white paper

* fine tip black felt-tip pen

For crazy stripes paper:

* square of corrugated card

* yellow paint * bright pink paint

* paintbrush

* large sheet of white paper

Flower print paper

1 Dip the end of the scouring pad into the saucer of red paint. Print it onto the paper. Repeat, leaving spaces between the prints, as shown on the finished wrapping paper.

2 Fill in the spaces in your design by making pink rose prints, following the instructions in step 1.

3 Use the felt-tip pen to draw a stem and a leaf, as shown here, to complete each flower.

Fingerprint chicks paper

1 Dip your finger in the saucer of yellow paint.

2 Press your finger onto a sheet of scrap paper to remove any excess paint.

3 Make a fingerprint on the large sheet of paper. Repeat steps 1 to 3 until your wrapping paper is covered with yellow fingerprints. Leave to dry.

4 Draw wings, feathers, legs and feet onto each chick, as shown here.

Crazy stripes paper

1 Brush yellow paint onto the corrugated card. Press it onto the paper. Repeat until the paper is covered with stripes. Leave to dry.

2 Brush bright pink paint onto the corrugated card. Press it onto the paper. Repeat to make a random pattern.

Party Bags

Make several of these decorated bags to use as party bags at your next birthday party, or use one instead of wrapping paper.

To make a bag you will need:

* pencil and thin white paper (for tracing the template)

* scissors

* double-sided sticky tape

AND

For the superhero bag:

* A4 sheet of orange paper

* blue paper

* yellow paper

* silver stars

For the princess bag:

* A4 sheet of green paper

* pink paper   * yellow paper

* stick-on craft jewels

1 Use thin white paper and a pencil to trace the party bag templates on pages 30 – 31. Cut them out. Tape them together along the sides marked X.

2 Place the complete template onto the coloured paper – orange for the superhero bag, green for the princess bag. Use pieces of masking tape to keep it in place. Draw around it with the pencil. Crease along all the fold lines and cut it out.

3 Take off the masking tape and the template. It should look like this.

4 Stick a strip of double-sided tape onto side flap A. Peel off the backing. Tape it onto side B.

5 Stick a strip of double-sided tape onto flap C. Peel off the backing.

6 Fold the flap up and stick it onto flap D.

Superhero

7 Press in the sides along the creases. Fold down the top flap.

1 Trace the lightning flash templates on page 31. Use the bigger one to cut out a blue flash and the smaller one to cut out a yellow flash. Glue the blue one onto an orange gift bag.

2 Glue the yellow flash onto the centre of the blue one, as shown. Stick on silver stars.

Princess

1 Trace and cut out the crown templates on page 31. Use them to cut out one pink and one yellow crown. Glue the pink crown onto the green gift bag.

2 Glue the yellow crown onto the centre of the pink crown. Add stick-on jewels.

Make an Envelope

An envelope is a lovely finishing touch to your homemade card. This way of making an envelope will work with all of the cards in this book.

You will need:

* a piece of paper (it needs to measure the same as the height of your card plus 6cm and twice the width of your card plus 8cm)

* card * glue * scissors
* ruler * pencil

1 Start by placing the card on the base of your sheet of paper, 4cm from the left-hand edge. Draw a line along each side of the card, twice the height of the card plus 6cm (**A**). Now draw lines 1cm from each side of the card and twice the height of the card plus 6cm (**B**).

2 Draw a line across the paper at the top of the card (**C**). Draw a parallel line 1cm above the top of the card (**D**). Draw a parallel line 2cm above the top of the card (**E**). Place the card on line E.

3 Draw a line across the top of the card (**F**). Draw a parallel line 1cm above the top of the card (**G**). Draw a parallel line 4cm above the top of the card (**H**).

4 Join up all the lines as shown in pink on the template on the right. Cut out around the shape.

5 Fold the paper along line **D**.

6 Fold the side flaps in and glue them in place.

7 Pop your card into the envelope and glue the top flap down or tuck the flap inside the envelope.

side flap

Card

side flap

Card

H

4cm

G

1cm

F

E

1cm

D

1cm

C

Card

4cm

A

A

4cm

B

1cm

B

1cm

Templates

Pop-up Ghost Card
Pages 8 – 9

Ghost

Bat

Bat

Castle

Monster Hug Card
Pages 6 – 7

Place on fold

Monster

Hand

Window

Monster Hug Card
Pages 6 – 7

Nose cone

Flames

Rocket Card
Pages 12 – 13

Rocket

Fold

Side flap A

Fold

Fold

X

Flap C

Fish

Blue flash

Water

Side flap B

Yellow crown

Pink crown

X

Fold

Fold

Swimming Fish Card
Pages 16 – 17

Goldfish bowl

Yellow flash

Fold

Flap D

Sweet Flower Card
Pages 14 – 15

Butterfly wings

Grass

Elephant print

Flower

Printed Wrapping
Page 21

Index

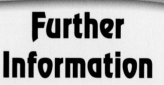

Further Information

Websites

For more card making ideas visit
www.redtedart.com/2012/05/11/20-
card-making-ideas-for-kids/

Books

Be Creative: Cards, Wrap and Tags by
Anna Claybourne (Franklin Watts)
Make and Use: Creative Cards by Rita
Storey (Wayland)
Usborne Art Ideas: Making Cards by
Fiona Watt (Usborne)